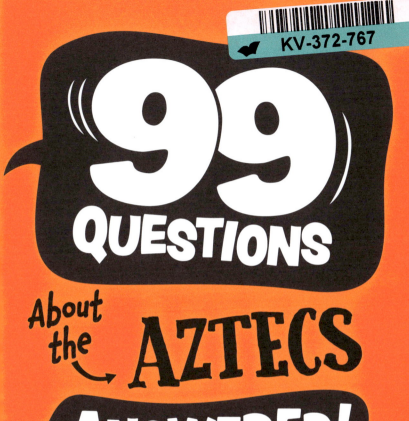

99 QUESTIONS

About the AZTECS

ANSWERED!

Annabel Savery

W
FRANKLIN WATTS
LONDON•SYDNEY

First published in Great Britain in 2024 by Franklin Watts
Copyright © Hodder and Stoughton Limited, 2024
All rights reserved.

Author and editor: Annabel Savery
Series designer: Rocket Design (East Anglia) Ltd
Consultant: Ian Mursell, Mexicolore (www.mexicolore.co.uk)

HB ISBN: 978 1 4451 8686 3
PB ISBN: 978 1 4451 8687 0

Franklin Watts
An imprint of
Hachette Children's Group
Part of Hodder & Stoughton
Carmelite House
50 Victoria Embankment
London EC4Y 0DZ

An Hachette UK Company
www.hachette.co.uk
www.hachettechildrens.co.uk
Printed in Dubai

Note to parents and teachers: every effort has been made by the Publishers to ensure websites are suitable for children, that they are of the highest educational value, and that they contain no inappropriate or offensive material. However, because of the nature of the Internet, it is impossible to guarantee that the contents of these sites will not be altered. We strongly advise that Internet access is supervised by a responsible adult.

Picture acknowledgements (bg = background, b = bottom, t = top, c = centre, r = right, l = left):
Shutterstock: Kurt Achatz 68, Afanasia 47, Marina Aknina 15, Alfaza Std 31, Black-Rhino1 37t, ArtMari18, Astarina 8c, Kiera Awayuki 3t, B.Illustrations 91, Arthur Balitskii 3c, Borsvelka 55, Viktoriia Chorna 61t, Cloudy Design 27, Dakin 64bg, Distrologo 12, Dn Br 38, Dolimac 60, Domira 19c, Anna Ermakova 41bl, Eroshka 6, Fargon 80, Flipser 58, Freud 48b, Peter Hermes Furian 73, Good Stock 86, graficriver_icons 34, Gwens Graphic Studio 20t, 20b, 46, HiToon 40, Maryia Ihnatovich 57b, Incomible 51bg, Irinia 43, Jaros 51b, Joeni91 61,Pavel K 30, Ilya Kalinin 36t, Kichikimi 57c, LarysArty 19b, Iastudio 50, Elena Latkun 54, Diana Latuga 37b, Leandro PP 71, Paul Lesser 70, LHF Graphics 78, Liubovart 7, Marina Loseva 48t, Magicleaf 28, Ismail El Makhloufi 88b, Mcarpzio 72, 92, Mhatzapa 65t, Milemil 26, Sasha Mitkalova 8b, More Vector 33, Morphart Creation 53, 81, Muse Stock 13, Neizu 52, Netsign33 39, nikiteev_konstantin 36b, NNNMMM 83,Nosyrevy 74, J Nutkins 84, Ollikeballoon 29b, Omarco 42, Onot 90, Owatta 9, 88t, Alexander_P 35b, Josep Perianes 59, Pranch 5, printstocker 25, Pyty 11,Guiseppe_R 14, Robuart 23, Ron and Joe 69, Rudall30 16, Pavlo S 29t,Ninelth Sandoval 24, Sararoom Design 9cr, Zdenek Sasek 17, 21b, Save nature 63, Anton Seredin 85, Shvetsova Design 89,Sidhe 66, Siridhata 45, Sokolfly 32, SoRad 82, Studio 77 FX vector 65c, The img 3b, Bodor Tivadar 49, Tsandra 41br, Vector Tradition 61b, 87, 95, Kelsey M Weber 44, Alex Woloski 67, Olga Yatsenko 22. Cover illustration & p10: Alan Brown
All additional design elements from Shutterstock or drawn by designer.

Every effort has been made to clear copyright. Should there be any inadvertent omission, please apply to the publisher for rectification.

The website addresses (URLs) included in this book were valid at the time of going to press. However, it is possible that contents or addresses may have changed since the publication of this book. No responsibility for any such changes can be accepted by either the author or the publisher.

All facts and statistics were up to date at the time of press.

THE AZTECS

It's time for a journey back through history to discover the secrets of the Aztecs! We'll find out about their incredible civilisation and whether they were really as bloodthirsty as some people think ...

WHERE DID THE AZTECS LIVE? YOU'LL FIND THE ANSWER IN QUESTION 5.

JUST WHO WAS MOCTEZUMA II? FIND OUT IN QUESTION 62.

DID AZTEC CHILDREN GO TO SCHOOL? THE ANSWER IS IN QUESTION 26.

WHO OR WHAT BROUGHT ABOUT THE END OF THE AZTEC ERA? TURN TO QUESTION 85 TO FIND OUT.

The letters **BCE** and **CE** appear in LOTS of history books, but what do they mean?

BCE stands for **BEFORE COMMON ERA** – so these dates are before the year 0. The higher the number, the older the date is; for example, 735 BCE comes before 734 BCE.

CE stands for **COMMON ERA** – so these dates are after year 0. The numbers rise higher as they become more recent.

WHO WERE THE AZTECS?

For a long time, people thought they were bloodthirsty warriors but now we know better. Today we know that the first Aztec tribe arrived in central Mexico in around 1325 CE. From their first settlements grew a civilisation of warriors but also farmers, engineers, inventors, artists, craftspeople and powerful kings.

Myths about Aztecs probably began with Spanish invaders, who were shocked by some of the Aztec's religious ceremonies, and Spanish tales were passed down through history. The Spanish destroyed the Aztec civilisation, and it has taken years of archaeology to find out the truth about these fascinating people.

Are you an Aztec?

No, I'm a Mexica!

AZTEC OR MEXICA?

Both of these words mean the same civilisation, but which is correct? Well, both!

The word Aztec was first used by historians writing about the peoples of Mexico. Today's historians will tell you that the Aztecs didn't call themselves 'Aztecs' though. They called themselves 'Mexica' (say *may-SHE-ka*).

For this book, we'll use the name Aztec as it is the term most people are familiar with. But if you are talking about Aztecs, it is good to understand that many people now call them the Mexica.

Make sense? Good, let's go on!

fact Mexica is the group name, Mexicatl refers to one person.

5

WHERE IS MESOAMERICA?

Mesoamerica describes the region we call Central America today – including the countries of Costa Rica, Nicaragua, Honduras, El Salvador, Guatemala and Belize – as well as central and southern Mexico. We use the term Mesoamerica to describe the land when the first civilisations lived there, before it was divided into the countries we know today.

WHO LIVED IN MESOAMERICA BEFORE THE AZTECS?

Hey, I was here first!

Some of the biggest civilisations that developed in Mesoamerica included the Olmec, Zapotec, Maya and the early Toltec. They shared many cultural and religious traditions and ideas.

WHERE DID THE AZTECS LIVE?

The Aztecs lived in central Mexico. Historians think that several tribes journeyed south at the same time to look for better farming land. They came from a mythical homeland somewhere far away in the north-west.

The area that the Aztecs settled in is called the Valley of Mexico. Here a vast inland sea, made up of smaller lakes, swelled in the rainy season and shrank back in the dry season.

The Aztecs and other tribes transformed the land around the lakes, creating cities and farming land. They spread across a large area, taking over more and more land. There were good farming lands, plains, rivers and mountains, and to the south there was tropical rainforest.

Swampland! Looks perfect!

fact Some people confuse the Aztec with the Maya people – the Maya civilisation began much earlier than the Aztecs and was based in a lowland region further to the south-east.

WHEN DID THE AZTECS LIVE?

We date the beginning of the Aztec Empire from around 1325 CE when they settled near Lake Texcoco. They grew in strength until 1519 when Spanish *conquistadors* arrived on their lands and destroyed much of their civilisation (more on this later, see Q86).

fact What was going on around the world in the 14th century?

★ England and France began the Hundred Years War – which actually lasted 116 years!

★ The Black Death pandemic spread around the world.

★ Powerful ruler Tamerlane conquered parts of Asia.

★ The enormous Mongol Empire was in decline.

★ Tennis was first played in England.

Thanks goodness someone invented tennis!

HOW DID THE AZTECS CHOOSE A PLACE TO SETTLE?

According to legend, the Aztecs journeyed from Aztlán ('place of the white herons') to find their first settlement. The migration took 150 years, as they stopped many times along the way, looking for the right place to live.

The Aztecs carried their god, Huitzilopochtli (see Q78), with them. He told them to look for an eagle, perched on a cactus, on top of a rock. They spotted the eagle on an island in Lake Texcoco. Even though it was empty swampland, they built a temple and began their settlement.

> Seen any snakes? I'm famished!

fact An eagle eating a snake on a cactus is the central image on the Mexican flag today.

HOW DID THE AZTEC EMPIRE GROW?

Grrrr!

When Aztecs founded their first settlement, they were just one small tribe among many. As they were small, they were ruled over by more powerful tribes.

The Aztecs managed to grow their settlement and create alliances with both the smaller and the more powerful tribes. They continued to grow and become more powerful, sending their armies out further across the Valley of Mexico to conquer more tribes and control more land. Each conquered tribe had to pay the Aztecs tribute (see Q15), which allowed them to grow HUGELY wealthy.

HOW BIG WAS THE AZTEC EMPIRE?

The Aztec Empire reached its largest extent in the early 1500s. At its biggest, it stretched from the Pacific Ocean in the west to the Gulf of Mexico in the east. It was thought to be around 135,000 square kilometres – just larger than the country of Greece today.

From its beginning as a small city-state, the Aztec Empire eventually ruled over some 400–500 other city-states. Its population is thought to have numbered 5–6 MILLION. It was one of the biggest Mesoamerican civilisations.

Mexico

GULF OF MEXICO

CARIBBEAN SEA

Maximum extent of the Aztec Empire

PACIFIC OCEAN

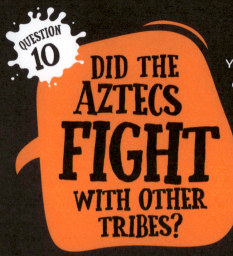

QUESTION 10

DID THE AZTECS FIGHT WITH OTHER TRIBES?

You bet! Small tribes were controlled by bigger city-states, which was probably pretty annoying.

When the Aztec civilisation was still quite small, they had to pay tribute to the powerful Tepanec people. Around 1428, the Aztec leader Itzcoátl formed the Triple Alliance with two other city-states: Texcoco and Tlacopan. They rose up against the Tepanec and won. This agreement allowed them to combine their armies, and so gain more land, power and influence. The Aztecs began to take over smaller tribes and settlements, becoming the dominant power themselves.

WHAT WAS THE
BIGGEST AZTEC CITY?

Tenochtitlán! Over the years, the first Aztec settlement became a vast metropolis, sprawling over 13 square kilometres. At its largest, historians think as many as 200,000 people lived in Tenochtitlán. At the same time, London had around 50,000 inhabitants, and Seville in Spain had around 60,000.

Tenochtitlán was packed with people, houses, marketplaces, temples, ball courts, palaces and gardens. Public buildings, such as temples and pyramids, were in the centre of the city. Around this area, housing spread out far and wide. Waterways ran through the city and people travelled around by canoe.

fact The Aztecs were wild about flowers and the city was full of gardens (see questions 37 and 38).

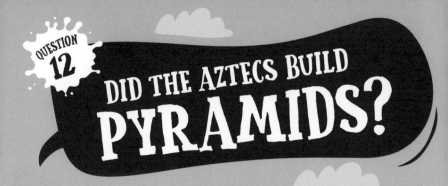

DID THE AZTECS BUILD PYRAMIDS?

Yes, building pyramids was an important part of Aztec culture. The first pyramids were actually quite small, and as the Aztecs became more powerful, they built bigger, better pyramids on top of the old ones!

Aztec pyramids had steps all the way up and temples on the top. The temples were believed to be home to the Aztec gods. The biggest pyramids were in the city centre, surrounded by an open square or plaza, where people could gather for celebrations and ceremonies. Pyramids were built tall and were painted white so that you could see them from far away.

I'm scared of heights!

WERE THE AZTECS GOOD AT PROBLEM-SOLVING?

Yes! The Aztecs were fantastic engineers. Without modern machines or materials, they built aqueducts (bridges that carry water) and canals to carry clean drinking water into Tenochtitlán. They also built causeways and canals to separate the salt and freshwater in Lake Texcoco, control the lake water level and to channel water to crops.

The Aztecs built their roads, pyramids and bridges all with human-power as they didn't have modern machines or big animals like horses to help them. Large stones were moved using ropes and rollers. They did, however, have hand tools for crafts and farming and simple machines for spinning and weaving cloth.

fact Fancy a home delivery of water? Sellers would collect the water piped into the city and take it to markets or homes.

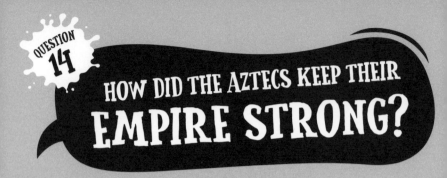

HOW DID THE AZTECS KEEP THEIR EMPIRE STRONG?

Firstly, by having a strong army. All Aztec men were part of the military and they also gained soldiers from some regions as a form of tribute (see Q15).

Secondly, by putting loyal nobles in charge of newly conquered city-states. Here they also built monuments and statues to spread their belief system (see Q74), laws and culture.

Thirdly, by making friends and family links. Aztec rulers sent gifts to rulers of distant regions to keep them happy, and also created ties by marrying the sons and daughters of these ruling families to Aztec nobles.

WHAT ARE TRIBUTES
AND WHY DID THE AZTECS NEED THEM?

A tribute was a payment made to people who had conquered you or ruled over you. If you paid tribute, the bigger state would leave you in peace!

Tribute payments made the Aztecs wealthy. Subject states paid tribute four times a year, and it could be paid in anything: gold, jade, feathers, animals, fabric or foods. With riches coming in from tribute states, the Aztecs could support their huge population and trade successfully. One of the codices (books) found by archaeologists shows that the Aztecs kept detailed records of tribute payments.

fact Tribute payments could be huge – such as 16,000 rubber balls or 240,000 pieces of cloth!

Just 239,986 pieces to go ...

WERE ALL AZTECS EQUAL?

Those pipiltin have all the fun!

All of Aztec society was organised into groups called *calpultin* (single *calpulli*) – a bit like a local neighbourhood today.

The two main divisions of society were the *pipiltin* – the nobility, and the *macehualtin* – everyone else! Within these groups there were eight levels. The nobility included the *tlatoque* (the rulers), high-ranking warriors, high priests and priestesses. The macehualtin were divided into middle and lower levels. The middle level included merchants, teachers and craftworkers. The poorer levels of Aztec society were made up of the free poor, such as part-time warriors who were also farmers and hunters, and unfree servants and enslaved people, who were owned by other people and worked without payment (see Q20).

WHAT WAS DAILY LIFE LIKE FOR THE AZTECS?

Your life as an Aztec depended on the family you were born into and which social group they belonged to (see Q16) – and what job you did. Whether you were a noble or not decided what rights you had, what clothes you could wear and even which cups you could use!

For everyone, hard work was well rewarded and respected. Daily life for most people meant working in the fields, marching off to war, or producing fine craftwork. Preparing food took up time each day and religious practices formed part of daily life too.

Er – can I use this cup?

fact
The Aztec day was divided into four sections – sunrise, mid-morning, noon and sunset – each announced with a conch-shell trumpet!

WHAT WAS IT LIKE TO BE
RICH IN AZTEC SOCIETY?

Being an Aztec noble could be pretty great! Nobles could own land and didn't pay taxes (unfair!). They were allowed to use fancy cups, enjoy flowers, drink cacao, wear cotton cloth and enter royal buildings. However, nobles were also expected to set a good example. If they broke the rules the punishments were severe.

WHAT WAS IT LIKE TO BE POOR AS AN AZTEC?

Basically, all the rules were reversed for the poor! They paid taxes and could not own land. They had to keep out of royal buildings, their pottery was plain and luxury goods were off limits – so no enjoying flowers! Punishments for the poorer classes could be less severe, but they were often performed in public.

HOW DID SOME AZTECS BECOME ENSLAVED?

Being enslaved was one of the punishments for committing a crime. Prisoners of war would also be enslaved. Sometimes, people could choose to go into slavery if they could not repay what they owed. These last slaves could not be sold or sacrificed (see Q81) ... unless they really misbehaved!

IS IT TRUE THAT A SLAVE COULD BECOME FREE BY STEPPING IN POO?

Bizarrely, yes! If you were a slave and could escape from your master in the slave market, make it to the ruler's palace without being caught by your master – or his son – and, at some point, step in human poo ... you would be freed! Whoop!

WHAT WAS LIFE LIKE FOR AZTEC WOMEN?

Both women and men had set roles in Aztec society. A woman's main role was to look after the home and to provide food for her family, but there were also plenty of jobs for women, such as priestess, midwife, matchmaker, market trader, fortune-teller, healer, weaver, potter and feather-worker.

There were ways in which women and men were equal: they could both own a house, be wealthy and control their own money. They were also both responsible for childcare once children were old enough to start learning about work. Women who died in childbirth were likened to warriors who died in battle. Their spirits were thought to help the Sun travel down from the midpoint in the sky to the sunset.

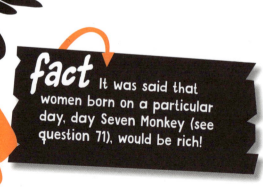

fact It was said that women born on a particular day, day Seven Monkey (see question 71), would be rich!

WAS DIVORCE
POSSIBLE FOR AZTECS?

Yes, it was, but couples were strongly encouraged to stay together. There may even have been special places where judges could hear marriage problems and try to help.

Before getting married, a couple made a list of the things they each brought to the marriage. The list was kept safe and used to divide their possessions again if the couple divorced. Fathers taught sons and mothers taught daughters, so children would be separated if a couple split up. Following a divorce, each person could re-marry if they wanted to.

WHAT WAS LIFE LIKE FOR AZTEC CHILDREN?

From the moment they were born, Aztec children were taught to be obedient and hardworking. Aztecs put a lot of effort into bringing their children up as useful members of society.

While children were still very young, they were raised by their mothers. When they were four, they were presented at the local temple where their ears were pierced and parrot feathers placed in their hair. This marked their first move into adult life. From this point, they would gradually take on more of their adult role. Adult tasks would start small – such as fetching water or collecting spilt grain.

fact The Aztecs were one of the first societies to educate all children. GO AZTECS! (More on school in question 26).

Do you like my feathers?

WERE AZTEC CHILDREN EVER PUNISHED?

YOU BET
THEY WERE!
Aztec parents wanted
to teach their children to
be hardworking, so laziness was
punished particularly severely.

Children could only be punished once
they had stopped being breast-fed
by their mothers – usually around
three years old. Before that, they
were believed to still be connected
to the sacred world. The worst
punishments might include being
poked with cactus spines or
wafted with smoke from
burning chillies ...

OUCH!

DID AZTEC CHILDREN GO TO SCHOOL?

Yes, but historians have different opinions about school age: some believe that children went to school from the age of five, others from the age of 15. All agree, though, that both boys and girls went to school. Boys and girls went to separate schools and schooling lasted for around one year.

A *calmecac* was a strict school, usually for the children of nobles. A *telpochcalli* was a school for everyone else. Many think that boys stayed at the school full time, but that girls would have returned home in the evening.

Boyz Rool!

Maybe, but they can't spell!

fact Sadly, we don't know much about what girls learnt at school because the people who wrote about schools were interested only in boys' education! HUMPH!

WHAT DID CHILDREN LEARN IN SCHOOL?

A calmecac school was attached to a temple and run by priests who taught religion, science, astronomy, art, maths, medicine, law, government, calendar systems, and more. As well as learning there was hard labour to do too, including farm work and making meals. All boys had to go out at night to pray and have a cold bath!

There was hard work at a telpochcalli, too, but also more freedom and fun. As well as chores, children learned religion and history, boys had military training and girls would learn crafts. At the end of the day there was music, singing and dancing.

I want to go to the other school!

WHAT TOYS
DID AZTEC CHILDREN HAVE?

Archaeologists have not found many Aztec toy artefacts. Although examples of small, wheeled animals have been found, it is thought that these were made specially to be burial objects (see Q84) as they show no signs of being used.

Historians think that children would have played with toy versions of objects that adults used in work – small bows and arrows for example. They would also have created playthings from the world around them, such as straw made into dolls or reeds made into whistles.

I love my straw dolls, but they are a bit scratchy!

DID THE AZTECS MAKE MUSIC?

Aztecs loved to make music! It was used by priests in ceremonies and enjoyed by rulers at court, as well as by people in their homes. Children could learn to dance and sing at a *cuicacalli* (house of song) and could also go to a *mecatlan* – music school.

Aztec instruments were made from natural materials: for example drums were made from wood with animal skin (hide) stretched over them. Whistles were made from clay or reeds, shells could be blown into, turtle shells and gourds could be made into drums, and even human skulls were used to make music!

TOK!

Ouch!

fact The Aztecs didn't have the same words to describe music as we do, so dancing was called 'singing with the feet'!

DID THE AZTECS PLAY SPORT?

They did, and by far the most important was the ball game *ullamaliztli*. Most Mesoamerican civilisations (see Q4) played a similar type of ball game – beginning in around 1700 BCE, and some people still play it today!

The ball game court, called a *teotlachco*, was shaped like a capital I – it had a central section with wide spaces at each end. Players had to keep the rubber ball moving by using just their hips! To the Aztecs this was much more than a sport, it was a ritual. Ball courts were often built near temples and even kings would take part!

fact Around 2,500 ancient Mesoamerican ball courts have been found!

WHAT JOBS
DID AZTECS DO?

Hard work was the name of the game for the Aztecs, and there was no shortage of jobs!

Being a farmer or a porter, called *tlamemehque*, were two of the most common jobs and kept the empire running. Aztec men often had two jobs: farmers in the rainy season, warriors in the dry. There were service jobs such as sweeping streets and transporting goods in canoes. Many people worked as traders in the busy markets and skilled craftwork included weaving baskets, sculpture, pottery and jewellery-making. People could also train as priests and priestesses, teachers, scribes and musicians.

The top jobs were the most important official roles, such as collecting tributes and being a city-state governor.

My arms ache!

WHAT GOODS DID THE AZTECS TRADE IN?

Markets were huge, bustling and busy – and sold everything from everyday goods such as food, tools and pots to luxury goods like jewellery, and feathers. Raw materials were for sale, including gold and resin. There were service traders such as potters and barbers, and enslaved people were also bought and sold.

As the Aztec Empire grew, so did the reach of their trading networks. The Aztecs exported salt, ceramics, jewellery, clothing and baskets. These were made with raw materials brought into their cities by trade and tribute.

fact It was said that you could hear the noise of the biggest market at Tlatelolco from around 4 kilometres away!

Keep the noise down!

DID THE AZTECS USE
MONEY?

The Aztecs didn't use coins, paper money or bank cards. Instead, trade was based on a system of bartering or swapping. One item might be swapped for something believed to be of the same value: for example, a canoe might be traded for a cotton cloak, but you would need 25 cloaks to buy a gold lip plug (see Q55)!

Cacao beans were also used for bartering. These are the beans that are used to make chocolate. They were used a little like coins and could be swapped for lower value goods – such as tomatoes or firewood. Field workers were paid in cacao beans and could use them to buy food.

Even if you didn't like chocolate, cacao beans were worth having!

fact In 1545, 1 cacao bean would buy an avocado. 20 cacao beans would buy a rooster!

HOW DID AZTECS TRAVEL?

The Aztecs had no big animals, such as horses or cows, and so all journeys on land were made by foot. On their many waterways, Aztecs travelled by canoe.

When waging war on another city-state, the army would travel on foot. As their army became so big, this was a huge operation and so support workers travelled along with the warriors.

Traders, called *pochteca*, and tlamemehque (porters) also travelled huge distances on foot. They would be as well-armed as the warriors because the roads could be dangerous.

WHY WERE AZTEC ROADS SO IMPORTANT?

Well-maintained roads meant that goods could flow into Aztec cities and armies could travel easily. As well as keeping trade going, road networks also allowed communication.

Along with the traders, warriors and porters who travelled on the roads were messengers. They were stationed at 4 kilometre intervals and worked like a relay team! *Paynani* carried messages from ordinary people. *Titantli* took messages between rulers or officials. They carried a fan and a staff to show who they were.

fact Traders were often also spies who brought news back to rulers from across the empire!

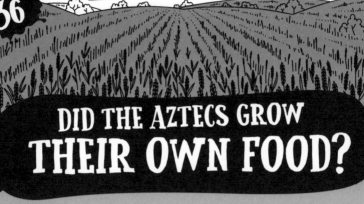

DID THE AZTECS GROW THEIR OWN FOOD?

Yes, they were excellent farmers. They had to make good use of their natural surroundings to feed their huge population! As their empire grew, food also came into their lands by trade and tribute.

Aztecs had rich soil and a warm climate – both were good for growing food. They knew how to put nutrients back into the soil and invented systems to bring water to their crops. They even managed to farm the swampy land around their island city Tenochtitlán by creating *chinampas* (see Q37) from the rich soil of Lake Texcoco.

fact To help keep their land fertile, the Aztecs around Tenochtitlán recycled their waste – food and human – back into the lake.

WHAT WERE CHINAMPAS?

Chinampas were key to the Aztecs being able to feed so many people. They were islands made from mud scooped up from the lake floor. Trees were planted to keep the mud in place, and walls, called dykes, channelled the water around the chinampas, keeping the crops watered. Chinampas allowed the Aztecs to farm what would otherwise have been swampland.

Where do you want this mud?

IS IT TRUE THAT THE AZTECS LOVED FLOWERS?

Yes, and they really loved them! They created floral garlands, posies and crowns and used them in ceremonies and at home. You name it, the Aztecs decorated it with flowers. There were also three months that celebrated – you guessed it – flowers!

DID THE AZTECS HAVE METAL TOOLS?

No, the main materials used to make tools were wood and hard volcanic stones such as obsidian and flint.

Obsidian was an important material for the Aztecs. This shiny, black volcanic glass could be shaped into a sharp edge. As well as being used in tools, it was also used to make weapons. Two other rocks, andesite and flint, were also used to make blades.

Wood was widely available and was used to make tools such as digging sticks, called *uictli*. These were poles with a long triangular blade on the end.

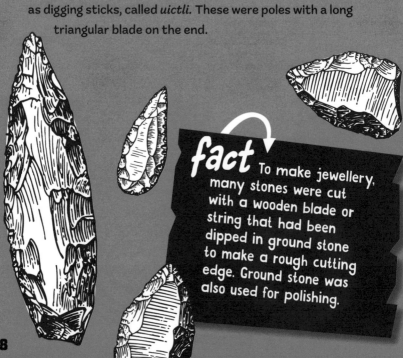

fact To make jewellery, many stones were cut with a wooden blade or string that had been dipped in ground stone to make a rough cutting edge. Ground stone was also used for polishing.

WHAT DID THE AZTECS EAT?

Aztecs ate the crops that they grew and food bought from markets. The wealthier you were, the more exotic the food you might eat. Aztecs ate meat from wild animals that they caught, and fish and waterfowl from lakes.

The plant, maize, which produces corn kernels or sweetcorn, was their most important food and was eaten at most meals. The kernels were ground into flour and made into thin cakes (*tortillas*), cooked in leaves to form dumplings (*tamales*), or made into a porridge called *atole*. These were eaten with other local foods such as squash, beans, tomatoes, avocados and chillies.

To the Aztecs, maize was just a-maize-ing!

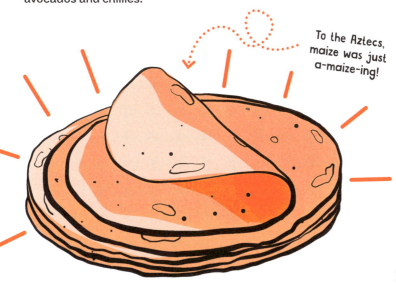

Us turkeys are well respected ... I think!

DID AZTECS KEEP ANIMALS?

Compared to other civilisations, the Aztecs did not keep many animals. They did not have farm animals, such as sheep or pigs, that were raised for meat or milk. The Aztecs did have dogs that they kept for companionship and protection, but they also hunted a different type of wild dog for meat. They kept turkeys for their eggs and meat.

Dogs and turkeys were well respected in Aztec culture. Turkeys, with their bald heads, were thought to represent long life. Dogs were a man's best friend – just like today – and the Aztecs particularly liked hairless dogs!

WHAT DID AZTECS COOK ON?

Inside, women cooked on a hearth: a simple fireplace in the centre of the home. Three stones were placed around the fire and were believed to contain the spirit of the fire god. The stones supported the *comalli*, a flat clay disk used for cooking on. There were also pots to cook stews in. Some houses had kitchens that were found outside, in a shared courtyard.

An essential piece of kitchen equipment was the *metate* – a stone used to grind corn into flour that could then be used to make other foods (see Q40).

Tra - la - la

I still don't like the look of that fire!

fact Women would sing or speak to maize before cooking it. They believed this would stop the maize from being afraid of the fire's heat!

41

WHAT DID AZTECS DRINK?

The Aztecs had a supply of clean drinking water, but there were also more delicious drinks available ...

From cacao beans, Aztecs made different types of chocolate drink flavoured with honey, chilli peppers, spices and vanilla. Luxury ingredients like these were drunk by wealthy people and given to celebrated warriors. A cheaper, simpler version of chocolate was drunk by ordinary people. Chocolate drinks were usually drunk cold, but there were hot versions too.

fact An alcoholic drink called *pulque* was made with fermented maguey plant. People were only allowed to drink four cups of it. The fifth cup was a bad idea!

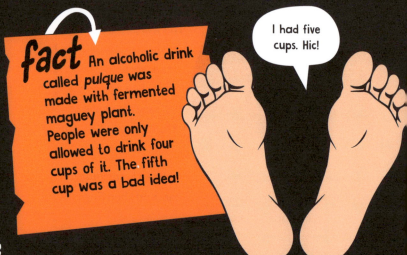

I had five cups. Hic!

DID THE AZTECS DISCOVER CHOCOLATE?

Nope! The discovery of this delicious bean was made by the Maya – a civilisation who lived before the Aztecs in a region to the south-east of Aztec lands. Maya traders came into contact with Aztecs and passed on their yummy knowledge!

I saw it first!

IS CHOCOLATE AN AZTEC WORD?

The word chocolate may come from *xocolatl* which is the word the Aztecs used for their chocolate drink. It may also have come from the word *choqui*, which means warmth.

The original Aztec word for cacao bean is *cacahuatl*. The Spanish mis-translated it as cacao, and then English traders misspelled cacao as cocoa!

WHAT TYPE OF HOUSES DID AZTECS LIVE IN?

Ordinary Aztec houses had just one room, with no chimney or windows. The walls were made of dried mud bricks, or sticks woven and covered with a type of plaster. Wooden beams made up the roof and were covered with a thatch of grass and other plants. Wealthier people had houses with stone walls and the really wealthy had homes with two floors.

Many homes were built around a shared courtyard that would have been used for relaxing and growing flowers. As the climate was warm, little time needed to be spent inside the home apart from sleeping and cooking.

Err, it's a bit dark in here!

DID THE AZTECS HAVE
MEDICINES?

The Aztecs had a range of treatments for illness, including herbal remedies, massage therapy and sweat baths. It is thought that around 85 per cent of Aztec treatments would have been effective, and that many would still be useful today.

Unwell Aztecs would go to a healer for help with all sorts of problems, including illnesses and home and relationship problems. Sweat baths (see Q48) were thought to help women before and after childbirth. The Aztecs had a great knowledge of medicinal plants and used them to treat anything from fear to bad breath! The Aztecs also had good treatments for battle wounds (see Q64).

fact Aztecs even had herbal remedies to help someone cross a river and for someone struck by lightning!

Ouch, I need a herbal remedy!

ZAP!

45

DID THE AZTECS KEEP CLEAN?

They did – and much more so than many other societies of the same time! The Spanish who invaded the Aztec Empire in the 1520s were shocked to find that Aztec ruler Moctezuma II bathed twice a day. Having a bath was not nearly so popular in Europe as it was in Mesoamerica!

Washing was quite normal for the Aztecs. They had plenty of clean water and liked to keep clean. They bathed in rivers, lakes or pools most days. The Aztecs didn't make soap but they did have two types of plant that they used to wash with.

fact Most homes had their own steam bath next to the house. The walls of a steambath were heated from the outside, and the bather threw water onto the hot walls to create steam.

DID AZTECS BRUSH THEIR TEETH?

Yes, evidence shows that the Aztecs rinsed their mouths after each meal and used a small root as a toothbrush. There were also different pastes that were used for cleaning and polishing teeth. One of these was made with ash and honey and was rubbed on with a cloth.

The Aztecs picked out food from between their teeth with small thorns or pieces of wood. They also had remedies for tooth decay that involved burning plants and ground stones, which were wrapped in a cloth and pressed onto the teeth.

WHERE DID AZTECS POO?

The Aztecs didn't have toilets in the home but they did have public toilets. These were cleaned regularly and the poo collected. Some public toilets were on canal bridges and the poo dropped down into canoes waiting below. Poo collectors then took it away to become fertiliser for farmland.

IS IT TRUE THAT WEE WAS SOLD AT MARKETS?

It is true! Wee, or urine, was a valuable product used both in the fabric dyeing process and also for many medical purposes. Households had a ceramic container to collect it in and it was sold in the markets. Nice!

WEE

WERE AZTEC CITIES
POLLUTED?

No, the opposite! Along with building public toilets, Aztec rulers also employed a thousand men to sweep the streets of Tenochtitlán every day. Animal, human and food waste was removed and taken to fertilise farmland. Sounds like Aztec cities were squeaky clean!

The Aztecs were also careful to collect and reuse other types of waste. Waste materials, such as fabric, were burnt in the city at night to give light.

fact There are no discoveries of Aztec rubbish dumps which suggests that their waste systems were very good!

WHAT DID THE AZTECS WEAR?

All women wore a wrap-around skirt called a *cueitl*, and a *huipilli* that slipped over the head like a T-shirt. Men wore a *maxtlatl*, a loincloth that wrapped around the waist and between the legs. Both men and women wore a cloak over their shoulders.

Clothes were different depending on whether you were rich or poor. Poorer people wore plain designs, while the wealthy wore colourful, embroidered clothing. *Ichtli* was the most common cloth and was made from the maguey plant. Cotton was imported and more expensive. It was mostly worn by the wealthy.

fact Some women's skirts were so brilliantly embroidered that they were passed down through generations.

A maguey plant

WERE THE AZTECS ARTISTS?

Aztec artists produced stone sculptures, beautiful pottery, mosaics, geometric patterns on fabric and fine metalwork. The images in Aztec art show elements of the world that surrounded them: people, plants and animals. Much art shows Aztec gods and goddesses (see Q77), who influenced their lives enormously.

Sculptures and ceramics were often painted in bright colours and formed part of religious ceremonies. Special stones such as amethyst, pearl and the most precious – jade – were carved into decorative shapes and brilliant blue turquoise was used in mosaics. Feathers were also cut up to create artworks, and items made from wood were decorated with beautiful carvings.

WHAT SORT OF JEWELLERY DID AZTECS WEAR?

Aztecs wore necklaces, beads and bracelets, and even nose ornaments! Plugs, made from precious metal and stones, stretched the soft skin of the earlobe or lip so that it grew around the plug – ouch! Some lip plugs were carved into shapes such as snakes.

However, the jewellery that people were allowed to wear depended on their social group. So even if an ordinary person owned some jewellery, they might not be allowed to wear it! Only nobles were allowed to wear gold and precious stones such as jade.

fact Lip plugs were awarded to young men when they took their first war captive, and to girls when they married.

WHAT SORT OF METALS DID THE AZTECS USE?

Aztec metalsmiths created beautiful items from gold and copper. Ores containing these metals were found outside Aztec lands, so they learned how to work these metals only when they explored further across Mesoamerica. There was no iron ore, so they did not have iron and steel as Europeans did.

Metal was melted in a furnace. The furnace was heated to an extremely high temperature by using a blow pipe. Objects were made by casting – pouring liquid metal into clay moulds – or created from sheets that had been hammered out. Beautifully decorated bells were some of the most common items cast.

fact Copper axe blades were used as a form of currency. They were valued higher than cacao beans but lower than cotton capes.

Blow! It needs to be really hot!

WERE FEATHERS WORTH MORE THAN GOLD TO THE AZTECS?

Yes – Aztecs were truly mad for feathers! Alongside the precious stone jade, feathers were the most valuable goods in the Aztec Empire. Many feathers were paid to the Aztecs in tribute from tropical lands to the south of their empire.

Most precious were the brilliant feathers of the quetzal and cotinga birds. The Aztecs were in awe of birds being able to fly, something no person could do! Feathers were part of the costume of the Aztec god Quetzalcoatl, the Feathered Serpent – whom they believed could soar like a bird between the sky, Earth and underworlds.

fact In a market, one feather cloak might be exchanged for 100 cotton capes.

HOW DID THE AZTECS USE FEATHERS?

It was all about the WOW factor!

Feathers were for the wealthy, powerful and important. They were used in jewellery, art and to create headdresses for warriors and priests. Rulers wanted to impress, and an enormous feather headdress, gleaming with gold and jade, would be certain to do that.

In the 18th century, an incredible headdress was found in an Austrian castle. It is around 116 centimetres high and made from 500 quetzal and blue cotinga tail feathers. Some believe this was the headdress of the Aztec ruler Moctezuma II or was given to the Spanish invader Cortés by Moctezuma II (see Q85 and Q62).

QUESTION
59

WHO WERE THE

AZTEC
RULERS?

The first Aztec tribes were ruled by elders – the oldest and wisest of the tribe. As the kingdom grew, the leaders became important and powerful kings.

The Aztecs called their kings *huey tlatoque* (singular *tlatoani*). The word tlatoani means 'he who speaks' – as the kings were believed to be both man and god.

During their civilisation, the Aztecs had nine kings. It was their job to grow the wealth and territory of the empire. As the role of king was passed down the male line, there were very few female rulers (see Q61).

DID AZTEC RULERS LIVE IN PALACES?

Yes, rulers lived in vast palaces, called a *tecpan calli*, right in the centre of the city. These had many rooms and were richly decorated – inside and out. There were rooms for business and rooms where the king and their extended family lived. There were also rooms for weapons and for storing tribute goods (see Q15). The remains of Moctezuma's II's palace lie underneath Mexico's national palace today!

Royal palaces were busy places, with many royal wives and children, noble guards, officials and warriors. There were caretakers who looked after the palace, as well as entertainers, cooks and servants.

fact Moctezuma II had gardens, a zoo, an aviary and ponds all within his palace grounds.

AVIARY   ZOO

WHAT WERE THE NAMES OF THE AZTEC KINGS?

These are the nine Aztec kings. Aztecs were given names from the natural world or important things around them.

Acamapichtli (Handful of Reeds) 1375 – 1395

Huitzilihuitl (Hummingbird Feather) 1395 – 1417

Chimalpopoca (Smoking Shield) 1417 – 1426

Itzcóatl (Obsidian Serpent) 1427 – 1440

Moctezuma I (Angry Lord) 1440 – 1469

Axayacatl (Face of Water) 1469 – 1481

Tizoc (The Bled One) 1481 – 1486

Ahuitzotl (Mythical Water Opossum) 1486 – 1502

Moctezuma II, also Moctezuma Xocoyotzin
(honoured young one) 1502 – 1520

Queens were important too, but rarely ruled alone. Two important queens were: Ilancueitl (old woman skirt!), thought to have been the wife of the first Aztec king; and Atotoztli (water bird), the daughter of Moctezuma I who is believed to have ruled before her son, Axayacatl.

WAS MOCTEZUMA II A GOOD KING?

Moctezuma was the last of the Aztec kings. He was feared but also respected by his people. Moctezuma was from a noble family and went to a calmecac school (see Q26). He was intelligent, faithful to the gods, and a good athlete. Moctezuma served as both a priest and warrior, and was a successful army commander at the time he was made king.

Throughout his rule, Moctezuma II ordered many successful campaigns, adding new lands to the empire that were rich in resources. But Moctezuma made a tragic mistake by not standing up to the Spanish when they arrived seeking gold and other treasures (see Q85).

We come in peace - sort of!

fact Rulers were allowed more than one wife! Moctezuma II had two 'official' wives and many others that he married to create political alliances with other tribes.

WHY WAS IT GOOD TO BE AN
AZTEC WARRIOR?

The Aztec Empire was built on successful military campaigns, so warriors were very important. Every male was given military training and success on the battlefield was well rewarded.

Success in the army was judged by how many captives each warrior could take – the more prisoners, the greater the reward. Men could improve their position in society and even gain a top job by being successful warriors.

He looks tough!

fact The army was organised into sets of 8,000 warriors, called *xiquipilli.* Each of these could be broken down into units of 400 men. Some historians believe that by the end of the Aztec Empire, the army would have had over 300,000 warriors.

HOW DID THE AZTECS TREAT WAR WOUNDS?

The Aztecs knew what they were doing when it came to battlefield first aid! First, wounds were washed with wee – which sounds icky but urine is surprisingly clean, as it contains little infection-causing bacteria. Special herbs would then be used to stop the bleeding and sap from the agave plant used to prevent infection.

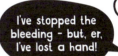

I've stopped the bleeding - but, er, I've lost a hand!

IS IT TRUE THAT AZTEC WARRIORS DRESSED AS JAGUARS?

Yes, but only the elite (top) ranks. Taking four enemy prisoners raised a soldier to the rank of 'jaguar and eagle'. To show their rank they wore animal skins and special headdresses. Their shields were also decorated with feathers and jaguar skins.

WHAT WEAPONS DID AZTECS HAVE?

The weapon that the Aztecs are best known for is a fearsome club called a *macuahuitl*. It was made from wood and shaped a bit like a cricket bat, but had sharp obsidian (see **Q39**) blades fixed into the edges. Other close-contact weapons included a club with a ball on the end and a hand-held lance.

The Aztecs also had a sling device called an *atlatl*, which hurled spears with obsidian points at the enemy. It could reach as far as 150 metres. There were other long-range weapons such as bows and arrows, darts and spears.

Deadly obsidian blades

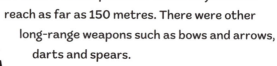

A macuahuitl

fact It was Aztec battle practice to injure rather than kill the enemy as they preferred to take live prisoners.

WHAT WERE AZTEC BATTLES LIKE?

A battle usually opened with insults! Elite warriors, called *cuahchique*, would mock the other side – saying they were weak and giving rude gestures. Women and children were allowed to join in too!

Then the army would fire aerial long-range weapons such as arrows and darts. After this, the two sides would charge, on foot, towards each other. Downhill charges were thought to be best, but this would have caused devastating injuries. Following the charge, the armies would spread out to begin hand-to-hand combat. Officers watched the battle carefully, sending in reserves of more warriors where they saw weak spots.

QUESTION 68

WHAT ARMOUR
DID AZTEC WARRIORS HAVE?

The Aztecs did not have metal armour. Instead, they wore sleeveless garments made from cotton cloth, padded inside with cotton fibres. These were worn by warriors who were going to be fighting hand-to-hand, at close range with the enemy. They were designed to protect the torso, where the body's vital organs, such as the heart, are.

Aztec warriors carried shields for protection. These were made from wood or reeds and covered in animal hide.

WHAT WERE FLOWER WARS?

Flower wars were battles arranged between different tribes. The aim for both sides was to gain prisoners of war and to train young soldiers. The word for these wars in Nahuatl is *xochiyaotl*, meaning 'war of flowers'. The link between flowers and wars were the soldiers' lives: full of glory but not lasting long.

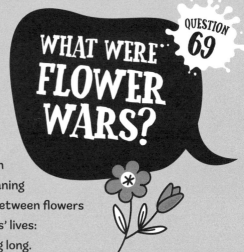

WHAT HAPPENED TO PRISONERS OF WAR?

SURPRISE GIFT

Prisoners of war were taken to live in Aztec lands and would either be given places in the captor's household or become enslaved. Some would be ritually sacrificed as a gift to the gods (see Q81). The better the warrior was, the greater the gift was believed to be.

FLINT

HOW DID THE AZTECS KEEP TRACK OF THEIR DAYS?

WIND

RAIN

The Aztecs followed two calendars. One divided the year into 18 20-day sections (*veintenas*), similar to our months – with five extra days to take the number of days to 365 (a full solar year).

DEATH

The other calendar was called the *tonalpohualli* – meaning 'the day count' – and had 260 days divided into 13 20-day sections. There were 20 day-signs, such as rain, eagle, jaguar, dog or water. People were given a proper name from the day they were born on, such as Five Wind. They were also given a personal name, such as Rain Flower.

RABBIT

JAGUAR

MONKEY

These two calendars ran alongside each other. It took 52 years for them to cycle through and line up with each other again.

GRASS

WHAT IS THE AZTEC
SUN STONE?

In 1790, workers discovered a huge circular stone slab buried under the Zócalo, Mexico City's main square. The slab is thought to have been carved during the reign of Moctezuma II and is known today as the Sun Stone.

In the centre of the Sun Stone is a carving of a face with the tongue sticking out. This is thought to be either the Aztec Sun god Tonatiuh or Earth god Tlaltecuhtli. Around him are pictures of the four creations (see Q75). In the next ring outward are the symbols for the Aztecs' 20 days (see Q71).

fact The Sun Stone is 3.5 metres wide and weighs an enormous 24 tons.

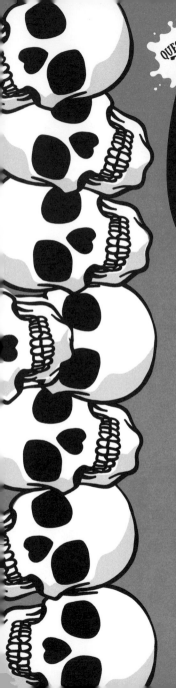

DID THE AZTECS REALLY MAKE TOWERS OF SKULLS?

Yes, scary stuff! The Spanish invaders who came to Aztec lands in 1520 told of gruesome towers of human skulls. In 2015, two skull towers were discovered beneath a building in Mexico City. They stood at each end of a skull rack, a *tzompantli*.

Towers of skulls and a skull rack stood outside the Templo Mayor in Tenochtitlán (see Q76), but skull racks have also been found near other temples or ball courts. The skulls came from people who had been sacrificed, but there were also some carved out of stone. Skull towers and racks were designed to frighten enemies, to show the Aztecs' power and success in war!

DID THE AZTECS FOLLOW A RELIGION?

Yes, Aztec religious beliefs ran through their whole lives, affecting all their behaviours. People had small altars where they could worship at home, and there were pyramids in each district, as well as the grand city pyramids.

The Aztec religion grew out of ancient Mesoamerican beliefs. They had many gods and goddesses who were related to each other. Many of these deities were seen as spirits of the natural world, such as rain and flowers. The Aztecs believed that everything on Earth had a life force, or *teotl*. They would pray to the spirits of trees for forgiveness when cutting them down, or to the spirits of the tools in their houses for help in their work.

Bit late now!

Sorry!

69

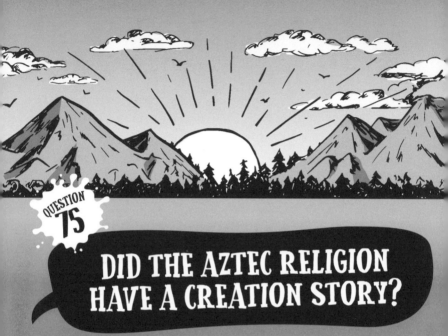

DID THE AZTEC RELIGION HAVE A CREATION STORY?

The Aztecs believed that they were living in the fifth creation of the Earth. The four previous ages – Sun of Jaguar, Sun of Wind, Sun of Fire and Sun of Rain – were each named after the force that had destroyed them. Aztecs believed that the Sun, Moon and humans were created at the beginning of the fifth era when a weak god, Nanahuatl, jumped into a great bonfire and became the Sun. His rival, Tecciztecatl, jumped in after him and became the Moon. Nanahuatl would not move across the sky until he had received a gift from the gods, so they sacrificed themselves to feed him. The movement of the two gods created day and night.

WHAT WAS THE TEMPLO MAYOR?

The Templo Mayor in Tenochtitlán was the Aztecs' most important temple. It was a vast pyramid with steps leading up to two smaller temples: one for Huitzilopochtli, the god of war; the other for Tlaloc, the god of rain (see Q77).

Construction of the Templo Mayor began when the Aztecs first settled on their lake island in 1325 and was added to by later rulers. Ceremonies for new rulers took place here, and many other religious and spiritual events. It was built in the centre of a square that was surrounded by a wall carved with snakes.

fact The Templo Mayor pyramid platform was a towering 60 metres high. That's the same height as ten giraffes!

HOW MANY GODS DID THE AZTECS HAVE?

Most experts would say there are over 100 Aztec deities. Around two-thirds of them were male, the rest were female, but some were both male and female. Each area, neighbourhood or town had its own special god or goddess, so who you worshipped depended partly on where you lived.

The deities influenced every part of Aztec life. Tlaloc – god of rain – was an important god to the Aztec people because they relied on farming to provide their food. Huitzilopochtli was the war god and they worshipped him hoping for success in war.

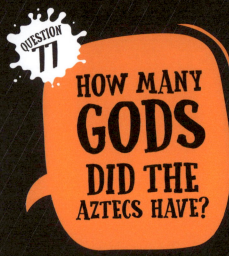

You want more rain?

Yes please!

WHO WERE SOME OF THE OTHER AZTEC GODS?

Ometeotl was the creator god and had four sons: Tezcatlipoca, Quetzalcoatl, Xipe Totec and Huitzilopochtli. Each of these represented a compass point and each also had a period of time dedicated to him in the Aztec tonalpohualli calendar (see Q71).

Quetzalcoatl was half-bird, half-serpent and an important god who influenced many things – from wind to jewellery! There was also Coatlicue the mother-Earth goddess, Tlaltecuhtli the Earth god, Xochipilli the god of flowers, Xipe Totec the god of Earth, regeneration and war, Mictlantecuhtli god of the dead, Centeotl the maize god, and Tonatiuh the Sun god – to name just a few!

Quetzalcoatl

fact Children who went to the calmecac school were taught to worship Quetzalcoatl, those who went to the telpochcalli school worshipped his rival Tezcatlipoca!

73

WHAT FESTIVALS
DID THE AZTECS CELEBRATE?

Festivals were linked to the Aztec calendars (see Q71) and each month celebrated a different god or goddess. There were feasts, parades, and often bloodletting and sacrifice (see Q81).

At festivals, people would dress up in costumes of the god or goddess being celebrated. In spring, people celebrated Chicomecoatl, goddess of farming, by making her offerings of food and creating dough figures of her. The autumn festival of Ochpaniztli celebrated the earth goddess Toci. She was linked to health and cleanliness, and so people swept roads, homes and courtyards. They also had pretend battles with brooms instead of weapons!

One of the most important celebrations was the New Fire Ceremony which took place on a mountaintop and celebrated the start of a new 52-year calendar cycle (see Q71).

Great party!

Happy New Cycle!

Eh?

WHAT WAS THE FESTIVAL OF IZCALLI?

The last 'month' in the Aztec calendar fell in January and February of the modern calendar. It was named Izcalli and it was a time of growth and rebirth. During this month, the Aztecs tried to encourage growth in everything from children to plants! They would take children by the neck and raise them upwards, just as maize grows.

During the Izcalli festival, some children would also have their ears pierced with cactus spines, OUCH!

fact Some sources say that the Aztecs believed that an earthquake was the spirit of the Earth moving and stretching, so they would stretch their children at this time too!

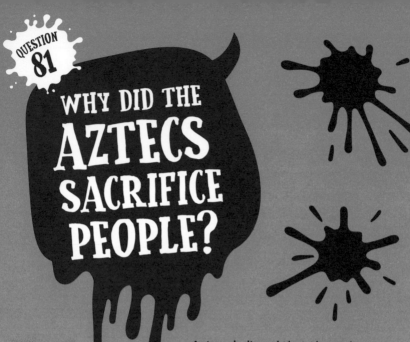

WHY DID THE AZTECS SACRIFICE PEOPLE?

Aztecs believed that the gods gave their lives to create the world (see Q75), and that they needed to repay this gift to keep the Sun rising each day. They did this by giving them many types of gift, including human blood.

Natural events, such as a drought or plague of locusts, could bring dangerous food shortages. The Aztecs believed that natural disasters were the gods' way of showing that they were unhappy. Sacrifices were performed at religious festivals and in times of trouble to try to please the gods. Usually, slaves or war captives were chosen for sacrifice.

WHAT ARE CHACMOOLS?

Chacmool is the name for a type of Aztec sculpture, where a figure holds a container for the human heart or blood following a sacrifice. The most well-known sculptures show a male figure, lying on his back with his torso raised. His hands hold a bowl that rests on his torso.

WERE THE AZTECS CANNIBALS?

Yes, but cannibalism was very limited. It formed part of Aztec beliefs that humans were part of the natural world, alongside their gods, animals, plants, mountains, rivers and streams, which all fed each other.

Sometimes when a captured warrior was sacrificed, the body was eaten by the captor's family, but not by the captor himself.

WHAT HAPPENED WHEN AN AZTEC DIED?

While some wealthy Aztecs were cremated (burned) after death, ordinary people were wrapped and buried in a seated position. People or their ashes were buried under their home.

The Aztecs believed that when a person died, they would go on a journey to the underworlds. Along the way there were nine challenges to face. To help with the journey, Aztecs were buried with the things that they would need: food and drink, 'tickets' made from paper, clothes, tools and weapons. People were dressed in clothes that represented their work and social status, and all had a jade bead placed in their mouth as 'travel money'.

ADMIT ONE

ADMIT ONE

- TICKET TO THE - UNDERWORLDS

fact The Aztecs believed there were nine underworlds and 13 heavens!

WHY DID THE AZTEC EMPIRE COME TO AN END?

In 1519, a Spanish fleet landed on the coast of Mexico looking for gold and other riches to take back to Spain.

At this time, the Aztec Empire was still expanding and Moctezuma II was in power. He thought at first that the Spanish were friendly; he gave them rich gifts and didn't challenge their progress through his lands.

The Spanish forces and their allies advanced through Aztec lands, eventually laying siege to the city of Tenochtitlán. The Spanish were victorious and went on to rule the area, destroying Aztec cities and enslaving Aztec people.

What a lovely chap, giving me all his gold!

WHO WERE THE CONQUISTADORS?

Hola!

In 1492, a Spanish adventurer called Christopher Columbus, reached the Americas. His tales of riches flowing from these countries made other adventurers want to explore them too. They were known as conquistadors, meaning 'they who conquer' in Spanish.

At this time, most European powers had started exploring by sea. Conquistadors came from all over Europe, but mainly from Spain and Portugal. They were funded by the Spanish rulers who demanded a fifth of all the gold they plundered. Most had been soldiers and knew how to fight and use weapons. Their aim was to conquer native peoples to steal their wealth.

fact Conquistadors were often given land in a conquered territory and put in charge of educating the enslaved local population and converting them to the Christian faith.

WHO WAS HERNÁN CORTÉS?

Anyone seen my trousers?

Hernán Cortés was the conquistador who led the Spanish forces against the Aztecs.

Cortés decided to go to sea in 1504 after seeing ships laden with riches coming to Spain from the west. In 1511, he helped conquer the island of Cuba and became rich and powerful. The governor of Cuba saw how powerful Cortés was becoming, and tried to prevent him setting out on an expedition to Mexico, but Cortés set sail before he could be stopped!

Cortés landed on the coast of Mexico in 1519 and was determined to take over the Aztec lands, especially when he saw that they were a wealthy civilisation.

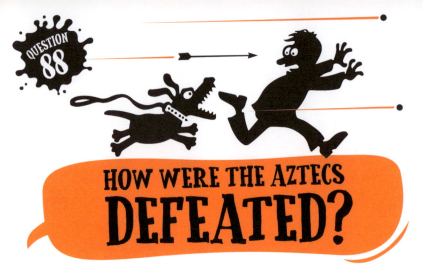

HOW WERE THE AZTECS DEFEATED?

The Aztec army was thought to number well over 300,000 men when Cortés and his forces arrived. The Spanish army was much smaller, but Cortés was able to make friends with many tribes who were tired of being controlled by the Aztecs and they joined his forces. Ruthlessly, Cortés killed any tribes that would not join him.

The Spanish attacked during the rainy season when the Aztecs were busy with farming. They brought weapons and animals with them that the Aztecs hadn't seen before: horses and mastiff dogs, guns, swords and crossbows. The Spanish also fought to kill, whereas the Aztecs wounded enemy soldiers in order to take them prisoner.

fact Among the killer weapons that the Spanish brought was disease. The Aztecs could not fight off European illnesses, such as smallpox, and many died from them.

WHO WAS **MALINTZIN?**
AND WHY WAS SHE SO IMPORTANT?

When Cortés arrived in Mexico he was given gifts by the Maya (see Q5), which included a women called Malintzin. She spoke not only Mayan but also Nahuatl – which was vital to Cortés' conquest of Aztec lands.

Malintzin and a Spanish friar, Guillermo de Aguilar, acted as interpreters for Cortés, supplying him with local knowledge and speaking with local tribes for him. It was tricky though: Cortés spoke Spanish to de Aguilar, who translated into Mayan for Malintzin, who then translated into Nahuatl for the tribes! By the time that Cortés met with Moctezuma II, Malintzin had learned Spanish and could translate directly.

Malintzin was multilingual!

fact Malintzin was known to the Spanish as Doña Marina or La Malinche.

WHAT HAPPENED IN THE SIEGE OF TENOCHTITLÁN?

When Cortés first arrived in Tenochtitlán, he was welcomed by Moctezuma II who let him live in a palace. When Cortés was out of the city, a Spanish general attacked and killed many Aztec nobles. Moctezuma II was also killed by the Spanish, who then fled from the city.

The disease smallpox, brought by the Spanish, killed almost half the population of Tenochtitlán. Months later, the Spanish laid siege to the city: they blocked supplies, including fresh water and food. In August 1521 the Aztecs were forced to surrender their biggest city to the Spanish invaders.

SMALLPOX

WHAT HAPPENED TO
TENOCHTITLÁN
AFTER THE SPANISH TOOK OVER?

After their victory, the Spanish destroyed the city. They took treasures, stole from homes, killed many thousands of people, and burned and destroyed everything that they could. Cortés built a new city on the ruins – Mexico City – and was named its governor.

The Spanish gradually took over Aztec lands, enslaving its people. Disease and the harsh conditions of enslavement eventually meant the overall population of the region fell from an estimated 25 million to 1.5 million.

fact Not all of the wealth that the Spanish sent home reached Spain. Some was stolen by British, French and other European privateers, or pirates!

HOW DO WE KNOW ABOUT
THE AZTECS?

Some of what we know of the Aztecs comes from books, called 'codices'. Though the majority of Aztec books were destroyed in the Spanish invasion, some were written later, possibly so that the Spanish could understand more of the Aztec culture and beliefs.

Other evidence comes from archaeology. This means looking at artefacts, often found buried in the ground, to work out what happened in human history and how our ancestors lived. Aztec temples and other sites reveal objects, such as flint knives, and other artefacts to tell us more about their behaviour and culture.

fact We also have books about the Aztecs written by the Spanish – but we have to be careful how we read these as the writers may have been more on the side of Spanish people, or did not fully understand Aztec culture.

DID THE AZTECS USE WRITING?

Yes – and no! The Aztecs used pictograms rather than letters and words as we do today. These small pictures represented people, places and actions. For example, footprints meant 'journey' and arrows or a sword meant 'war'. The pictures worked as prompts for stories, songs or rituals and were shown at the same time as someone spoke. People who wrote or drew books were called *tlacuilos*, or scribes.

The Aztecs wrote hundreds and hundreds of books that they called *amoxtin*. Their books recorded not only their beliefs and stories, but also kept records of their tribute systems.

fact There are just two surviving books that scholars think might be Aztec: the *Codex Borbonicus* and the *Tonalamatl Aubin*.

DID THE AZTECS MAKE PAPER?

The Aztecs made their own paper from tree bark or cactus fibres. They soaked the fibres in water and flattened them with stones. Some paper was also made from dried animal skin. Vast amounts of paper were brought into Tenochtitlán as tribute (see Q15).

WERE AZTEC BOOKS THE SAME AS OURS?

Books made following the Spanish invasion were designed in a similar way to European books: with pages joined at the spine and the pictograms read from left to right. Books created by the Aztecs from before this time, however, were made from long pieces of material that were folded back and forth into a zigzag. They didn't always read from left to right, either.

WHICH WERE THE BEST AZTEC INVENTIONS?

The Aztecs were ingenious in their technology, in medicine and in the making of their crafts. Today, we still admire their chinampas farming system and the aqueducts that brought fresh water into the city of Tenochtitlán.

The Aztecs also discovered that small insects that live on the prickly pear cacti produce a substance, now known as cochineal, that could be used to dye cloth a deep rich red. This insect proved important to the Spanish economy for around 300 years, as they kept the source of the dye a secret.

The Aztecs are also thought to have been the first to produce popcorn and chewing gum!

CAN ANY AZTEC BUILDINGS BE SEEN TODAY?

Most Aztec buildings were destroyed in the Spanish invasion. However, there are a few Aztec sites that can be visited today.

The buildings that remain are the larger structures, such as pyramids. The ruins of a double-temple pyramid can be seen at Tenayuca, a town close to Tenochtitlán. This is an incredible site as it was taken over and extended by different civilisations, including the Toltec, Chichimec and Aztec. The remains of the Templo Mayor – the most important Aztec pyramid – can also be seen in Mexico City.

fact Beneath a building in Mexico City, archaeologists have found the palace of Emperor Axayácatl, which was also used by Spanish conquistador Hernán Cortés.

WHAT LANGUAGE DID THE
AZTECS SPEAK?

The Aztecs spoke Nahuatl, the language of the earlier Toltec civilisation, which spread across much of Mesoamerica. As the Aztec Empire grew so large and powerful, their language became the *lingua franca* of a wide region – which is a fancy way of saying everyone spoke it even if they had another language that they used every day!

lingua franca

DO WE USE ANY AZTEC WORDS TODAY?

After the Spanish invasion, many Nahuatl words entered European languages. Words such as avocado, chilli, chocolate, ocelot (a wild cat), tomato, axolotl and chipotle all come from Nahuatl.

Today the official language of Mexico is Spanish, but native languages, including Nahuatl, are taught and used in schools, too. Around 1.5 million people in Mexico speak Nahuatl.

Avacado is just one of many words we get from the Aztecs.

AN AZTEC TIMELINE

1168 – 1325 Nomadic Aztec tribes journey south and settle on Lake Texcoco

1375 – 1426 Reigns of Acamapichtli, Huitzilihuitl, Chimalpopoca

1427 – 1440 Reign of Itzcoatl

1428 Triple alliance between city-states of Tenochtitlán, Texcoco and Tlacopan

1440 – 1469 Reign of Moctezuma I

1469 – 1481 Reign of Axayacatl

1481 – 1486 Reign of Tizoc

1486 – 1502 Reign of Ahuitzotl

1502 – 1520 Reign of Moctezuma II

1519 Arrival of Spanish in Yucatán, Mexico

1521 Siege of Tenochtitlán, surrender of the Aztecs to Spanish leader Cortés

99 QUESTIONS

The dates here give approximate time periods for each historical period. Historians generally agree on these dates, but new information is being found all the time!

SERIES TIMELINE

STONE AGE BRITAIN
2.5 million to 2,500 years ago

ANCIENT EGYPTIANS
3000 BCE — 30 BCE

ANCIENT GREEKS
1200 BCE — 323 BCE

BRONZE AGE BRITAIN
2,500 BCE — 800 BCE

SHANG DYNASTY
1600 — 1046 BCE

IRON AGE BRITAIN
800 BCE — 43 CE

ROMANS
753 BCE — 500 CE

ANCIENT MAYA
200 — 1519

VIKINGS
750 — 1066

SONG DYNASTY
960 — 1279

KINGDOM OF BENIN
1180 — 1897

AZTECS
1325 — 1521

GLOSSARY

archaeology the study of human history by looking at evidence such as buildings and tools; an archaeologist studies archaeology

artefact an object made by humans that can tell us about human history

astronomy the study of the Sun, Moon, stars and other natural objects in space

axolotl a salamander (creature similar to a lizard) that lives in the water, native to North America

aviary a place where birds are kept

bacteria very small organisms (living things) that can cause illness and disease

barter to swap or exchange goods

causeway a raised strip of land that crosses a swamp or other waterway

ceramics items, such as pots, vases or cups, made from clay that has been baked hard

chipotle a dried, smoked chilli often used in Mexican cooking

conquistadors 16th century Spanish explorers and treasure-seekers

cremation a ceremony or funeral service in which a person's dead body is burned

deity a god or goddess

dominant holding power or influence over someone or something

fertilise to add substances to farmland that make it good for growing crops

friar a member of a group within the Roman Catholic church

gourd a large round fruit with a hard skin, which can be made into a container

infant a baby or very young child, often meaning a child that cannot yet feed itself

jade a hard stone that can be shaped into ornaments, usually green, but can be other colours such as white

maguey a plant in the agave family, with long spiky leaves

Mesoamerica describes the region we call Central America today – including the countries of Costa Rica, Nicaragua, Honduras, El Salvador, Guatemala, Belize – as well as central and southern Mexico

migration a long journey from one place to another

nutrient a substance that helps a plant or animal grow

obedient able to do as instructed; a child who does as they are told

resin a sticky liquid found in trees that dries hard

sacrifice to kill a person or animal in a religious ceremony as an offering to a deity

scribe a person whose job it is to write or draw

siege a way of attacking a town; where the army surrounds the town and stops supplies getting to it

tribute a payment made to a more powerful state, to prevent them from attacking you

AZTEC WORD BANK

CALMECAC school for noble children

CALPULLI neighbourhood or local area

CHINAMPAS farming land made from raised lake mud

COMALLI a flat clay disk for cooking on

CUICACALLI house of song

METATE a stone used to grind corn kernels into flour

MEXICA the name that the Aztecs called themselves

PAYNANI messengers for ordinary people

PIPILTIN nobility

POCHTECA traders

TELPOCHCALLI school for common children

TEOTLACHCO a ball court

TITANTLI official messengers

TLAMEMEHQUE porters

TLATOQUE rulers (single: tlatoani)

UICTLI digging sticks

ULLAMALIZTLI the ball game

FURTHER INFORMATION

BOOKS

So You Think You've Got It Bad: A Kid's Life In the Aztec Age
Chae Strathie, Nosy Crow, 2021

Explore!: Aztecs
Izzi Howell, Wayland, 2018

WEBSITES

A great website with everything you could want to know about the amazing Aztec civilisation.
www.mexicolore.co.uk/aztecs/kids

A good introduction to the Aztecs from the Britannica encyclopedia.
kids.britannica.com/students/article/Aztec/273040

INDEX

OTHER TITLES IN THE 99 QUESTIONS SERIES

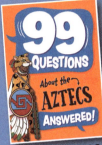

978 1 4451 8686 3

978 1 4451 8690 0

978 1 4451 8692 4

978 1 4451 8694 8

978 1 4451 8697 9

978 1 4451 8698 6

978 1 4451 8702 0

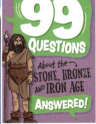

978 1 4451 8705 1

978 1 4451 8706 8

978 1 4451 8701 3